P9-CQO-831

Who carved Love
        and placed him by
this fountain,
        thinking
he could control
        such fire
with water?

*Zenodotos*

Where there is a woman there is magic. If there is a moon falling from her mouth, she is a woman who knows her magic, who can share or not share her power. A woman with a moon falling from her mouth, roses between her legs and tiaras of Spanish moss, this woman is a consort of the spirits.

*Ntozake Shange*

### *Searching for the One in My Dreams*

There is no Compass of Dreams. North is not the home of lost birds. Red is not the color of neighing horses. You do not ride a gray wolf into my circle.

Nothing is where or what it's expected to be: not your name on my tongue dissolving into sweet syllables. Not whiskey-talk around Coyote's fire. Not your strong body I boast to know.

Like any dreamer, I am lost. You could step out of my dreams in a T-shirt and jeans, singing about owls and I wouldn't know you. Your face is not used to being loved. It is only an image of what my hands want to cup.

White birds across the dark leaves of fall: this is you. Your name is a red branch. Your eyes have been the western twilight. Your mouth knows my passionate direction. Though you be the only rain on a high plateau, I will find you.

*Anita Endrezze*

## Song for a Dark Voice

My black sun, my
Odessa sunflower,
spurs of Tartar gold
ring at your ankles,
you stand taller before me than ten
towers of Jerusalem.

Your tongue has found
my tongue, peonies
turn their profusion towards
the lamp, it is you that burn there,
the Black Sea sings you awake.

Wake the violoncellos of Lebanon,
rub the bows with cedar resin,
wake the Tundra horsemen
to hunt tigers.
       Your skin
tastes of the salt of Marmora,
the hair of your body casts
its net over me.
       To my closed eyes
appears a curved
horizon where darkness
dazzles in your light. Your arms
hold me from falling.

*Denise Levertov*

## One Night

The room was poor and squalid,
hidden above the dubious tavern.
From the window you could see the alley
filthy and narrow. From below
came the voices of some workmen
playing cards and carousing.

And there on the much-used, lowly bed
I had the body of love, I had the lips
the voluptuous and rosy lips of ecstasy—
rosy lips of such ecstasy, that even now
as I write, after so many years!
in my solitary house, I am drunk again.

*C. P. Cavafy*
*translated by Rae Dalven*

What chord did she pluck in my soul
that girl with the golden necklace
& ivory breasts
whose body ignited the river,
she who rose like the moon
from her bathing
& brushed back the ebony hair
that fell to her waist
& walked off
into the twilight dark —
O my soul,
what chord did she pluck
that I am still trembling.

*Steve Kowit*
*after Chandidas*

8

Since first I heard his name
it has overcome my heart
& thrown my life into confusion—
I cannot get enough. I whisper
it all day & half the night.
It is intoxicating.
I have grown so drunk upon it
I have lost all semblance of control
& am responsible for nothing
that I do— especially today,
when my addiction took a fatal turn
for I discovered where he lives
& when he is likely to be home,
& how can an innocent girl
defend herself against that?
May heaven protect me!
If his name alone is heady enough
to drive me insane,
God knows what will happen tonight
when I taste his lips.

*Steve Kowit*
*after Dwija Chandidas*

### Cancionero

Come at dawn, beloved.
Come at dawn.

Lover, I want you.
Come at the dawn of day.

Lover, I love you.
Come at the break of day.

Come at the break of day.
Don't bring anybody.

Come at the light of dawn.
Come, all alone.

*Anonymous*

Not speaking of the way,
Not thinking of what comes after,
Not questioning name or fame,
Here, loving love,
You and I look at each other.

*Yosano Akiko*
*translated by Kenneth Rexroth*

Black hair
Tangled in a thousand strands.
Tangled my hair and
Tangled my tangled memories
Of our long nights of love making.

*Yosano Akiko*
*translated by Kenneth Rexroth*

In intimacy there's a secret place
even passion cannot penetrate,
even when lips touch in horrible silence
and love rips the heart like paper.

There friendship, there years of fury
are meaningless.
There slow sensuality
leaves the soul alone.

Those who want intimacy go mad,
and those finding it are ravaged.
Do you understand—why my heart stops
under your hand?

*Anna Akhmatova*
*translated by Mary Maddock*

Consuming me, she moved away,
The golden goddess.
The glow of her skin ripped open her sari
As her form fought with the azure blue dress.
How would I hold
The lightning in my eyes? —
I could no longer watch.

Her eyes were restless,
Bracelets jingled.
The bees flew drunk with the flavor of her fragrance,
And she walked away like an elegant swan.
Her hips were firm as the pride of a lioness
But blending with the sweetness of honey.
What nectar glistened in her smiling eyes!

*Chandidas*

I ne'er was struck before that hour
    With love so sudden and so sweet.
Her face it bloomed like a sweet flower
    And stole my heart away complete.

My face turned pale as deadly pale,
    My legs refused to walk away,
And when she looked "what could I ail?"
    My life and all seemed turned to clay.

And then my blood rushed to my face
    And took my sight away.
The trees and bushes round the place
    Seemed midnight at noonday.
I could not see a single thing,
    Words from my eyes did start;
They spoke as chords do from the string
    And blood burnt round my heart.

Are flowers the winter's choice?
    Is love's bed always snow?
She seemed to hear my silent voice
    And love's appeal to know.
I never saw so sweet a face
    As that I stood before:
My heart has left its dwelling-place
    And can return no more.

*John Clare*

14

## Madrigal

Like the Idalian queen,
Her hair about her eyne,
With neck and breast's ripe apples to be seen,
At first glance of the morn
In Cyprus' gardens gathering those fair flowers
Which of her blood were born,
I saw, but fainting saw, my paramours.
The Graces naked danced about the place,
The winds and trees amazed
With silence on her gazed,
The flowers did smile, like those upon her face;
And as their aspen stalks those fingers band,
That she might read my case,
A hyacinth I wished me in her hand.

*William Drummond*

Mother, do not expect me till late.
Tho I like the boy's company
his car's an old hunk of tin
with a penchant for puttering out
a hundred miles from nowhere.
By the time we get the thing rolling again
my hair will be down,
my clothes wrecked,
I'll be scratched in a dozen spots
& the sun will be up.

*Steve Kowit*
*after the Sanskrit*

All night we lay in each other's arms.
The words gushed forth
as if language itself
had come into being
there,
with our love.
We talked about everything . . .
nothing . . .
not even dawn stopped us.

*Steve Kowit*
*after Bhavabhuti*

Others saw him too
as he stood at the edge
of the ripening field
& asked simply if
there was work. He
who held a canvas satchel
over his shoulder
came, he said,
from the land where
the summer west wind
makes flute music
out of the little holes
that the bees bore
in the swaying bamboo,
& the cold water
falling over the rocks
is the music of drums,
& monkeys shriek
when a peacock dances
about on one of the hills
like a young woman.
    Friend,
is it possible
I am the only one
of all those
who saw him that day
who tosses about in my bed,
night after night,
with a grief nothing
has caused, & my arms
clutching the darkness?

*Steve Kowit*
*after the Tamil*

17

### On the New Road

red sumac presses
against the windshield,
tires moan

Your wife dreams
you are guilty,

I button and unbutton
what I feel

*Lyn Lifshin*

18

### *It Is True*

Oh, what an effort it is
to love you as I do!

For love of you, the air,
my heart
and my hat hurt me.

Who will buy of me
this ribbon I have
and this grief of white
linen to make handkerchiefs?

Oh, what an effort it is
to love you as I do!

*Frederico Garcia Lorca*
*translated by Harriet De Onis*

## *A Young Wife*

The pain of loving you
Is almost more than I can bear.

I walk in fear of you.
The darkness starts up where
You stand, and the night comes through
Your eyes when you look at me.

Ah, never before did I see
The shadows that live in the sun!

Now every tall glad tree
Turns round its back to the sun
And looks down on the ground, to see
The shadow it used to shun.

At the foot of each glowing thing
A night lies looking up.

Oh, and I want to sing
And dance, but I can't lift up

My eyes from the shadows: dark
They lie spilt round the cup.

What is it? — Hark
The faint fine seethe in the air!

Like the seething sound in a shell!
It is death still seething where
The wild-flower shakes its bell
And the skylark twinkles blue —

The pain of loving you
Is almost more than I can bear.

*D. H. Lawrence*

Drunk as drunk on turpentine
From your open kisses,
Your wet body wedged
Between my wet body and the strake
Of our boat that is made out of flowers,
Feasted, we guide it — our fingers
Like tallows adorned with yellow metal —
Over the sky's hot rim,
The day's last breath in our sails.

Pinned by the sun between solstice
And equinox, drowsy and tangled together
We drifted for months and woke
With the bitter taste of land on our lips,
Eyelids all sticky, and we longed for lime
And the sound of a rope
Lowering a bucket down its well. Then,
We came by night to the Fortunate Isles,
And lay like fish
Under the net of our kisses.

*Pablo Neruda*
*translated by W. S. Merwin*

## *Wild Vines*

Beneath a willow entwined with ivy,
we look for shelter from the bad weather;
one raincoat covers both our shoulders—
my fingers rustle like the wild vine around
    your breasts.

I am wrong. The rain's stopped.
Not ivy, but the hair of Dionysus
hangs from these willows. What am I to do?
Throw the raincoat under us!

*Boris Pasternak*
*translated by Robert Lowell*

### "O My Love the Pretty Towns"

O my love
The pretty towns
All the blue tents of our nights together
And the lilies and the birds glad in our joy
The road through the forest
Where the surly wolf lived
And the snow at the top of the mountain
And the little
Rain falling on the roofs of the village
O my love my dear lady
The world is not very big
There is only room for our wonder
And the light leaning winds of heaven
Are not more sweet or pure
Than your mouth on my throat
O my love there are larks in our morning
And the finding flame of your hands
And the moss on the bank of the river
And the butterflies
And the whirling-mad
Butterflies!

*Kenneth Patchen*

## *Lovers' Play*

This morning my lady caught a mole
in the fields
as she was strolling over his hill.
Now she explains the furry
black thing in her palm
and offers her earth-scented hands
for foolish sniffing.
She has been my love for a long time
and one spring she'll be my wife.
She loves me
is simple like sunlight
sleeps in my arms on summer afternoons
and, when she is startled out of sleep,
she bites my lips hard
among birds.
Their beaks wide open,
astonished at the song.

*Miklós Radnóti*
*translated by Nicholas Kornblum*

### *I Knew a Woman*

I knew a woman, lovely in her bones,
When small birds sighed, she would sigh back at them;
Ah, when she moved, she moved more ways than one:
The shapes a bright container can contain!
Of her choice virtues only gods should speak,
Or English poets who grew up on Greek
(I'd have them sing in chorus, cheek to cheek).

How well her wishes went! She stroked my chin,
She taught me Turn, and Counter-turn, and Stand;
She taught me Touch, that undulant white skin;
I nibbled meekly from her proffered hand;
She was the sickle; I, poor I, the rake,
Coming behind her for her pretty sake
(But what prodigious mowing we did make).

Love likes a gander, and adores a goose:
Her full lips pursed, the errant note to seize;
She played it quick, she played it light and loose;
My eyes, they dazzled at her flowing knees;
Her several parts could keep a pure repose,
Or one hip quiver with a mobile nose
(She moved in circles, and those circles moved).

Let seed be grass, and grass turn into hay:
I'm martyr to a motion not my own;
What's freedom for? To know eternity.
I swear she cast a shadow white as stone.
But who could count eternity in days?
These old bones live to learn her wanton ways:
(I measure time by how a body sways).

*Theodore Roethke*

The minute I heard my first love story
I started looking for you, not knowing
how blind that was.

Lovers don't finally meet somewhere.
They're in each other all along.

*Rumi*
*translated by John Moyne and Coleman Barks*

There's a strange frenzy in my head,
of birds flying,
each particle circulating on its own.
Is the one I love *every*where?

*Rumi*
*translated by John Moyne and Coleman Barks*

## *In the Arc of Your Mallet*

Don't go anywhere without me.
Let nothing happen in the sky apart from me,
or on the ground, in this world or that world,
without my being in its happening.
Vision, see nothing I don't see.
Language, say nothing.
The way the night knows itself with the moon,
be that with me. Be the rose
nearest to the thorn that I am.
I want to feel myself in you when you taste food, in the arc
of your mallet when you work.
When you visit friends, when you go
up on the roof by yourself at night.

There's nothing worse than to walk out along the street
without you. I don't know where I'm going.
You're the road and the knower of roads,
more than maps, more than love.

*Rumi*
*translated by John Moyne and*
*Coleman Barks*

### A Well-Worn Story

In April, in April,
My one love came along,
And I ran the slope of my high hill
To follow a thread of song.

His eyes were hard as porphyry
With looking on cruel lands;
His voice went slipping over me
Like terrible silver hands.

Together we trod the secret lane
And walked the muttering town.
I wore my heart like a wet, red stain
On the breast of a velvet gown.

In April, in April,
My love went whistling by,
And I stumbled here to my high hill
Along the way of a lie.

Now what should I do in this place
But sit and count the chimes,
And splash cold water on my face
And spoil a page with rhymes?

*Dorothy Parker*

## Recuerdo

We were very tired, we were very merry —
We had gone back and forth all night on the ferry.
It was bare and bright, and smelled like a stable —
But we looked into a fire, we leaned across a table,
We lay on a hill-top underneath the moon;
And the whistles kept blowing, and the dawn came
    soon.

We were very tired, we were very merry —
We had gone back and forth all night on the ferry;
And you ate an apple, and I ate a pear,
From a dozen of each we had bought somewhere;
And the sky went wan, and the wind came cold,
And the sun rose dripping, a bucketful of gold.

We were very tired, we were very merry —
We had gone back and forth all night on the ferry.
We hailed, "Good morrow, mother!" to a shawl-
    covered head,
And bought a morning paper, which neither of us
    read;
And she wept, "God bless you!" for the apples and
    pears,
And we gave her all our money but our subway fares.

*Edna St. Vincent Millay*

Her eyes in sleep
afterward

her body my love

sounds she uttered then
without meaning

yet not meaningless

my heartbeat even now
echoing them.

*Sanskrit*
*translated by W. S. Merwin*
*and J. Moussaieff Masson*

32

I have always been sorry
Our words were so trivial
And never matched the depths
Of our thoughts. This morning
Our eyes met,
And a hundred emotions
Rushed through our veins.

*Liu Yü Hsi*
*translated by Kenneth Rexroth*

### Class Conscious

I put my hands on the table
right after you noticed the hammers
I wear for earrings.
An accidental gesture
            sort of.
The hands that wield a hammer
I wanted to show you
so there'd be no illusions
about me
            tough woman
            tough hands.
I didn't want you to get the wrong idea
about me
            looking so feminine in some parts.
*What you see*
my hands say for me
*is what you get.*

I put my hands on the table
tentative
proud        sort of
hoping you are one of the ones
who likes a working hand

and scared you're not.

*Kate Braid*

## *A Spring Night in Shokoku-Ji*

Eight years ago this May
We walked under the cherry blossoms
At night in an orchard in Oregon.
All that I wanted then
Is forgotten now, but you.
Here in the night
In a garden of the old capital
I feel the trembling ghost of Yugao
I remember your cool body
Naked under a summer cotton dress.

*Gary Snyder*

I am not yours, not lost in you,
    Not lost, although I long to be
Lost as a candle lit at noon,
    Lost as a snowflake in the sea.

You love me, and I find you still
    A spirit beautiful and bright,
Yet I am I, who long to be
    Lost as a light is lost in light.

Oh plunge me deep in love—put out
    My senses, leave me deaf and blind,
Swept by the tempest of your love,
    A taper in a rushing wind.

*Sara Teasdale*

"What do you want?" I said.
the night all almond flowered.
"You've got a smudge on your cheek," I said
& tried to rub it off.
her skin felt cold-smooth to my fingers.
I kissed both cheeks      her nose
her lips—just tasted
did not enter in.

And what did I expect?
eternal youth!
to be a flaming Bodhisattva
the lotus under my heels
my heels carpeted above the waters!

I am a flaming Bodhisattva.
I touched her cheek      all almond flowered.
kissed her mouth.
entered the flaming waters
my heels floating above the carpet.

What did I expect
the night being almond shaped & flowered?

*John Gill*

### Rhetorical Questions

Why don't you call me?

Why don't you not even bother to call me
after all this time?

Why don't you get into your filthy Buick
with its two bad tires right now?

Why don't you drive here
thinking only of me for as long as it takes
and get out in front of the house
where I rent a small room
which has gotten away from me?

Why don't you come to the door,
ask for me by name,
and look for me coming
down the stairs?

You could open your coat
even though it's raining,
and take me in

because it is.

*Brenda Brooks*

### *Love Song*

Sweep the house clean,
hang fresh curtains
in the windows
put on a new dress
and come with me!
The elm is scattering
its little loaves
of sweet smells
from a white sky!
Who shall hear of us
in the time to come?
Let him say there was
a burst of fragrance
from black branches.

*William Carlos Williams*

39

### *Love, It Is Time*

Love, it is time I memorized your phone
Number and made it a part of what I keep
Not in a black book but in living bone
Of fingertips that dial you in my sleep.
Time that the Roman wires of my heart
Lead all to you like artery or vein
Or tourist roadmap or a fever chart,
Since you are central now to my love's brain.
Teri, I have your number in my blood,
Your name is red and racing in my pulse
And all my nerves are ringing as they should
Through the night's black and sweet umbilicus
Connecting our two lives with strings of words
That you send back this spring like flights of birds.

*Karl Shapiro*

Last night I vowed anew, I swore an oath by your life,

That I would never remove my eyes from your face; if
you smite with the sword, I will not turn from you.

I will not seek the cure from any other, because my
pain is of separation from you.

If you should cast me into the fire, I am no true man
if I utter a sigh.

I rose from your path like dust; now I return to the
dust of your path.

*Rumi*
*translated by A. J. Arberry*

It is a bright house;
not a single room is dim.

It is a house which rises high
on the cliffs, open
as a lookout tower.

When the night comes
I put a light in it,
a light larger than the sun and the moon.

Think
how my heart leaps
when my trembling fingers
strike a match in the evening.

I lift my breasts
and inhale and exhale the sound of love
like the passionate daughter of a lighthouse keeper.

It is a bright house.
I will create in it
A world no man can ever build.

*Fukao Sumako*
*translated by Kenneth Rexroth and Ikuko Atsumi*

## Woman

When you were a girl
you could sting
like the thorn of a wild blackberry.
Your foot, too, little savage,
you wielded as a weapon.

You were hard to take.

                 Now still young
You are still lovely, the threads
of years and sorrow bind together
our souls, and make them one. No longer
under the jet-black strands that my fingers
gather in do I fear
the little white faunlike keen-pointed ear.

*Umberto Saba*
*translated by Thomas G. Bergin*

43

### Unclench Yourself

Open, love, open.
I tell you we are able
I tell you we are able
now and then gently
with hands and feet
cold even as fish
to curl into a tangle
and grow a single hide,
slowly to unknit all other skin
and rest in flesh
and rest in flesh entire.
Come all the way in, love,
it is a river
with a strong current
but its brown waters
will not drown you.
Let go.
Do not hold out
your head.
The current knows the bottom
better than your feet can.

You will find
that in this river
we can breathe
we can breathe
and under water see
small gardens and bright fish
too tender
too tender
for the air.

*Marge Piercy*

### *Gloire de Dijon*

When she rises in the morning,
I linger to watch her;
Spreads the bath-cloth underneath the window
And the sunbeams catch her
Glistening white on the shoulders,
While down her sides the mellow
Golden shadow glows as
She stoops to the sponge, and the swung breasts
Sway like full-blown yellow
Gloire de Dijon roses.

She drips herself with water, and the shoulders
Glisten as silver, they crumple up
Like wet and falling roses, and I listen
For the sluicing of their rain-dishevelled petals.
In the window full of sunlight
Concentrates her golden shadow
Fold on fold, until it glows as
Mellow as the glory roses.

*D. H. Lawrence*

## Waiting

My love will come
will fling open her arms and fold me in them,
will understand my fears, observe my changes.
In from the pouring dark, from the pitch night
without stopping to bang the taxi door
she'll run upstairs through the decaying porch
burning with love and love's happiness,
she'll run dripping upstairs, she won't knock,
will take my head in her hands,
and when she drops her overcoat on a chair,
it will slide to the floor in a blue heap.

*Yevgeny Yevtushenko*
*translated by Robin Milner-Gulland and Peter Levi*

And in the end I'll say —
goodbye, don't commit yourself to love.
I'm going crazy. Or else I climb
to a higher level of madness.

The way you loved! — You sipped at
ruin. That's not quite it.
The way you loved! — You ruined it,
but did it so clumsily.

The cruelty of a miss. You won't be
forgiven. My body is alive,
wanders and sees the white world
but is hollow.

My head still manages
a little work. But my hands fall limp at my sides
and like a sparse flock of birds, obliquely,
all smells and sounds leave me.

*Bella Akmadulina*
*translated by Mary Maddock*

Ah —you thought I'd be the type
You could forget,
And that praying and sobbing, I'd throw myself
Under the hooves of a bay.

Or I would beg from the witches
Some kind of root in charmed water
And send you a terrible gift —
My intimate, scented handkerchief.

Damned if I will. Neither by glance nor by groan
Will I touch your cursed soul,
But I vow to you by the garden of angels,
By the miraculous icon I vow
and by the fiery passion of our nights —
I will never return to you.

*Anna Akhmatova*
*translated by Judith Hemschemeyer*

Little fleece of my flesh
that I wove in my womb,
little shivering fleece,
sleep close to me!

The partridge sleeps in the clover
hearing its heart beat.
My breathing will not wake you.
Sleep close to me!

Little trembling blade of grass
astonished to be alive,
don't leave my breast.
Sleep close to me!

I who have lost everything
am now afraid to sleep.
Don't slip away from my arms.
Sleep close to me!

*Gabriela Mistral*

### *She Gets Up at Dawn Like Bakers*

My love is a slender woman with wide hips.
I flew on a plane. From above she looks small.
Even as a pilot, I'd do her honor,
She washes her own clothes,
the suds quiver on her arm.
She kneels as in prayer when she scrubs the floor
but later bursts out laughing.
Her laughter is an apple whose skin you bite into.
She gets up at dawn to knead the dough
like bakers who're uncles of ovens.
They watch over us with their long shovels.
The flour scatters,
settles on their broad, free chests.
The flour rests like my love in her fresh-smelling bed
after she has washed the dishes
and hugged my heart clean.

My wife will be just like her
when I'm a grown man
and marry like Father.

*Attila József*
*translated by Nicholas Kornblum*

### On Second Thought
*Last night's inspiration:*
*write an erotic poem*

Now I sit here
cold early morning light
hard chair

Your body, familiar as my own
passes the window
working the garden
in sweaty
earth stained garb
old flop-brimmed hat

You are no help
conjure no visions
of flame tongued nights
mad paroxysms of lust
or Sutrian delights

Right now a second cup of coffee
a ripe and succulent peach
tempt me to leave this task

luring my senses with a pull
stronger than your proximity

Perhaps this is all
that need be said
If you came in, touched me
took me to our bed
my breasts would swell
my nipples rise as they do now

To hell with peaches
there is sweeter juice
let someone else write poems
Come in
there's better planting to be done

*Maude Meehan*

Wild Nights—Wild Nights!
Were I with thee
Wild Nights should be
Our luxury!

Futile—the Winds—
To a Heart in port—
Done with the Compass—
Done with the Chart!

Rowing in Eden—
Ah, the Sea!
Might I but moor—Tonight—
In Thee!

*Emily Dickinson*

## Thieves Bay

I drive you to the ferry after not enough said
and you kiss me, still silent.
You are leaving with something of mine.

Later, I walk in the fog for hours.

Only the rocks are clear, and the water
and the ducks, calling to each other
constantly, keeping in touch.

*Kate Braid*

## *Since There's No Help*

Since there's no help, come let us kiss and part—
Nay, I have done, you get no more of me;
And I am glad, yea, glad with all my heart,
That thus so cleanly I myself can free.
Shake hands for ever, cancel all our vows,
And when we meet at any time again,
Be it not seen in either of our brows
That we one jot of former love retain.
Now at the last gasp of Love's latest breath,
When, his pulse failing, Passion speechless lies,
When Faith is kneeling by his bed of death,
And Innocence is closing up his eys,
    —Now if thou would'st, when all have given him over,
    From death to life thou might'st him yet recover.

*Michael Drayton*

Enough, Catullus, of this silly whining;
What you can see is lost, write off as lost.
Not long ago the sun was always shining,
And, loved as no girl ever will be loved,
She led the way and you went dancing after.
Those were the days of lovers' games and laughter
When anything you wanted she approved;
That was a when the sun really shone.
But now she's cold, you too must learn to cool;
Weak though you are, stop groping for what's gone,
Stop whimpering, and be stoically resigned.
Goodbye, my girl. Catullus from now on
Is adamant: he has made up his mind:
He won't beg for your favor like a bone.
You'll feel the cold, though, you damned bitch, when men
Leave *you* alone. What life will you have then?
Who'll visit you? Who'll think you beautiful? Who'll
Be loved by you? Parade you as his own?
Whom will you kiss and nibble then?
                                    Oh fool,
Catullus, stop this, stand firm, become stone.

*Catullus*

*translated by James Michie*

## *To His Mistress Going to Bed*

Come, Madam, come, all rest my powers defy,
Until I labor, I in labor lie.
The foe oft-times having the foe in sight,
Is tir'd with standing though he never fight.
Off with that girdle, like heaven's Zone glistering,
But a far fairer world encompassing.
Unpin that spangled breastplate which you wear,
That th'eyes of busy fools may be stopped there.
Unlace yourself, for that harmonious chime,
Tells me from you, that now it is bed time.
Off with that happy busk, which I envy,
That still can be, and still can stand so nigh.
Your gown going off, such beauteous state reveals,
As when from flowery meads th'hill's shadow steals.
Off with that wiry Coronet and shew
The hairy Diadem which on you doth grow:
Now off with those shoes, and then safely tread
In this love's hallow'd temple, this soft bed.
In such white robes, heaven's Angels used to be
Received by men; Thou Angel bringst with thee
A heaven like Mahomet's Paradise; and though
Ill spirits walk in white, we easily know,
By this these Angels from an evil sprite,
Those set our hairs, but these our flesh upright.

Licence my roving hands, and let them go,
Before, behind, between, above, below.
O my America! my new-found-land,
My kingdom, safeliest when with one man mann'd,
My Mine of precious stones, My Empirie,
How blest am I in this discovering thee!
To enter in these bonds, is to be free;
Then where my hand is set, my seal shall be.
    Full nakedness! All joys are due to thee,
As souls unbodied, bodies uncloth'd must be,
To taste whole joys. Gems which you women use
Are like Atlanta's balls, cast in men's views,
That when a fool's eye lighteth on a Gem,
His earthly soul may covet theirs, not them.
Like pictures, or like books' gay coverings made
For lay-men, are all women thus array'd;
Themselves are mystic books, which only we
(Whom their imputed grace will dignify)
Must see reveal'd. Then since that I may know;
As liberally, as to a Midwife, shew
Thy self: cast all, yea, this white linen hence,
There is no penance due to innocence.
    To teach thee, I am naked first; why then
What needst thou have more covering than a man.

*John Donne*

### Ratio

Thinking about you
is to being with you
as the state of coma
is to waking wide,
as a particle second
is to an hour
raised to the highest
possible power.

*Lillian Morrison*

I wish I were close
To you as the wet skirt of
A salt girl to her body.
I think of you always.

*Yamabe No Akahito*
*translated by Kenneth Rexroth*

He was really her favorite
student dark and just
back from the army with
hot olive eyes, telling her of
bars and the first
time he got a piece of
ass in Greece or was it
Italy and drunk on some strange
wine and she thought
in spite of his dangling
pronoun (being twenty-four and
never screwed but in her
soft nougat thighs) that he
would be a
lovely experience.
So she shaved her legs up high
and when he came
talking of footnotes she
locked him tight in her
snug black file cabinet where
she fed him twice a day and
hardly anyone noticed
how they lived among bluebooks
in the windowless office
rarely coming up for sun or the
change in his pronoun or the
rusty creaking chair
or that many years later
they were still going to town in
novels she never had time to finish

*Lyn Lifshin*

62

i want to say the words that take you back there.
wherever you'd like to be.
was there a lamp in the window?
a bowl of fruit you could really eat?
plants hanging from the ceiling in pots in the bathroom?
what was there you liked,
there, where
you'd like to be again?

for me it's steam on the windows
snow delicately waiting on the dark twigs.
the moon between clouds &
the smell of someone i love.
crisp taco all drippy with oil.
love it love it love it love it

*Alta*

## Acknowledgments

Every effort has been made to trace the ownership of all copyrighted material and to secure the necessary permissions to reprint these selections.

**Yamabe No Akahito** "I wish I were close…," from *One Hundred Poems from the Japanese*, translated by Kenneth Rexroth. All rights reserved. Reprinted by permission of New Directions Publishing Corp.

**Yasano Akiko** "Not speaking of the way…" and "Black hair…," from *One Hundred Poems from the Japanese*, translated by Kenneth Rexroth. All rights reserved. Reprinted by permission of New Directions Publishing Corp.

**Anna Akhmatova** "Ah—you thought I'd be the type…," translated by Judith Hemschemeyer. Reprinted by permission of Zephyr Press.

**Alta** "i want to say the words that take you back there…," reprinted by permission.

**Kate Braid** "Class Conscious" and "Thieves Bay," from *Covering Rough Ground*. Reprinted by permission of Polestar Press Ltd., Vancouver, B.C.

**Brenda Brooks** "Rhetorical Questions" from *Blue Light In the Dash*. Reprinted by permission of Polestar Press Ltd., Vancouver, B.C.

**Anita Endrezze** "Searching For the One in My Dreams," from *at the helm of twilight*. © 1992 Anita Endrezze. Reprinted by permission of Broken Moon Press.

**Steve Kowit** All translations reprinted by permission.

**Denise Levertov** "Song for a Dark Voice," reprinted by permission of New Directions Publishing Corp.

**Lyn Lifshin** "On the New Road" and "He was really her favorite…," reprinted by permission.

**Liu Yu Hsi** "I have always been sorry…," from *One Hundred More Poems from the Chinese*, translated by Kenneth Rexroth. Copyright © 1970 by Kenneth Rexroth. Reprinted by permission of New Directions Publishing Corp.

**Frederico Garcia Lorca** "It Is True," translated by Harriet De Onis. Reprinted by permission of New Directions Publishing Corp.

**Maude Meehan** "On Second Thought," reprinted by permission

**Lillian Morrison** "Ratio," from *Overheard in a Bubble Chamber and other science poems*. Copyright © 1981 by Lillian Morrison. Reprinted by permission of Marian Reiner for the author.

**Boris Pasternak** "Wild Vines," from *Imitations*, translated by Robert Lowell. Reprinted by permission of Farrar, Straus & Giroux, Inc. Book Publishers.

**Marge Piercy** "Unclench Yourself," from *Living in the Open*. Reprinted by permission of The Wallace Agency.

**Miklós Radnoti** "Lover's Play," from *Turmoil in Hungary*. Reprinted by permission of New Rivers Press.

**Rumi** "Last night I vowed anew…," from *Mystical Poems of Rumi*, by Arberry. Reprinted with permission of The University of Chicago Press.

**Umberto Saba** "Woman," from *Contemporary Italian Poetry*, edited by Carlo Golino. Copyright © 1962 by The Regents of the University of California. Reprinted by permission of the University of California Press.

**Sanskrit Love Poetry** translated by W. S. Merwin and J. Moussaieff Masson. Copyright © 1977 by Columbia University Press. Reprinted with permission of the publisher.

**Karl Shapiro** "Love, It Is Time," from *White-Haired Lover*. Copyright © 1967 by Karl Shapiro. Reprinted by permission of Wieser & Wieser.

**Fukao Sumako** "It is a bright house…," from *Women Poets of Japan*, translated by Kenneth Rexroth and Ikuko Atsumi. Copyright © 1977 by Kenneth Rexroth and Ikuko Atsumi. Reprinted by permission of New Directions Publishing Corp.

**William Carlos Williams** "Love Song," reprinted by permission of New Directions Publishing Corp.

**Yevgeny Yevtushenko** "Waiting," from *Yevgeny Yevtushenko: Selected Poems*, translated by Robin Milner-Gulland and Peter Levi. Penguin Modern European Poets.